Baby Animals

Richard Northcott

T0346983

Name _____

Age _____

Class _____

OXFORD

UNIVERSITY PRESS

OXFORD

UNIVERSITY PRESS

Great Clarendon Street, Oxford OX2 6DP

Oxford University Press is a department of the University of Oxford.
It furthers the University's objective of excellence in research, scholarship,
and education by publishing worldwide in

Oxford New York

Auckland Cape Town Dar es Salaam Hong Kong Karachi
Kuala Lumpur Madrid Melbourne Mexico City Nairobi
New Delhi Shanghai Taipei Toronto

With offices in

Argentina Austria Brazil Chile Czech Republic France Greece
Guatemala Hungary Italy Japan South Korea Poland Portugal
Singapore Switzerland Thailand Turkey Ukraine Vietnam

OXFORD and OXFORD ENGLISH are registered trade marks of
Oxford University Press in the UK and in certain other countries

ISBN-13: 978 0 19 440081 7

Printed in China

The publisher would like to thank the following for their kind permission to reproduce the following:
Alamy Stock Photo pp 2(collies/GROSSEMY VANESSA), 4 (kitten/PetStockBoys),
8 (rabbits/Ernie James), 10 (lioness/Mark Boulton), 12 (gorilla/Eric Gevaert), 14 (owls/
Wild Pictures); **Shutterstock** p6 (lambs/Rob Kemp).
Cover image courtesy of Juniors Bildarchiv GmbH/Alamy Stock Photo

With thanks to Sally Spray for her contribution to this series

📖 Using the book

1 Begin by looking at the first story page (page 2). Look at the picture and ask questions about it. Then read the story text under the picture with your students. Use section 1 of the CD for this if possible.

2 Teach and check the understanding of any new vocabulary. Note that some of the words are in the **Picture Dictionary** at the back of the book.

3 Now look at the activities on the right-hand page. Show the example to the students and instruct them to complete the activities. This may be done individually, in pairs, or as a class.

4 Do the same for the remaining pages of the book.

5 Retell the whole story more quickly, reinforcing the new vocabulary. Sections 2 and 3 of the CD can help with this.

6 If possible, listen to the expanded story (section 4 of the CD). The students should follow in their books.

7 When the book is finished, use the **Picture Dictionary** to check that students understand and remember new vocabulary. Section 5 of the CD can help with this.

💿 Using the CD

The CD contains five sections.

1 The story told slowly, with pauses. Use this during the first reading. It may also be used for "Listen and repeat" activities at any point.

2 The story told at normal speed. This should be used once the students have read the book for the first time.

3 The story chanted. Students may want to chant along with the story.

4 The expanded story. The story is told in a longer version. This will help the students understand English when it is spoken faster, as they will now know the story and the vocabulary.

5 Vocabulary. Each word in the **Picture Dictionary** is spoken and then used in a simple sentence.

This dog has two puppies.
They are very cute.

Connect.

one puppy

two puppies

three puppies

four puppies

five puppies

six puppies

This is a kitten.
A kitten is a baby cat.

Connect.

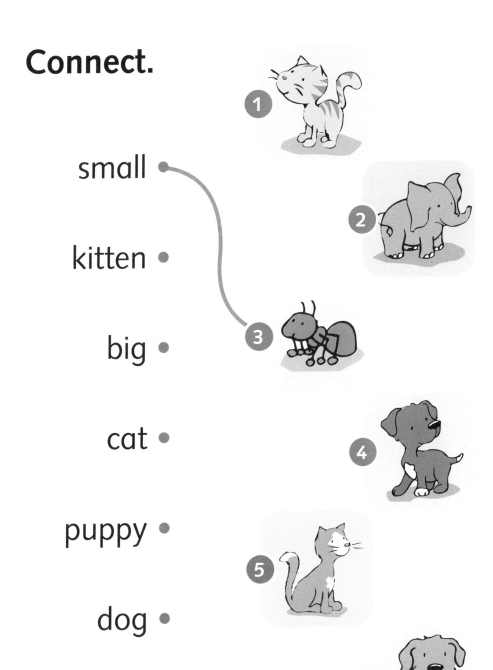

small

kitten

big

cat

puppy

dog

This is a mother sheep.
She has two lambs.

Circle yes or no .

1. This is a sheep. ~~yes~~ no

   yes
   no

2. This is a dog. yes
   no

3. This is a puppy. yes
   no

4. This is a cat. yes
   no

5. This is a kitten. yes
   no

6. This is a dog. yes
   no

7. This is a lamb. yes
   no

These are baby rabbits.
They have long ears.

Circle yes or no .

1. I can see four rabbits.   yes / (no)

2. I can see three rabbits.   yes / no

3. The rabbits are black.   yes / no

4. The rabbits are small.   yes / no

5. The rabbits are big.   yes / no

6. They have long ears.   yes / no

7. They have pink eyes.   yes / no

8. They have blue noses.   yes / no

This lion has two cubs.
Lion cubs like to play.

How many?

① How many rabbits?   `5`

② How many cubs?

③ How many kittens?

④ How many puppies?

⑤ How many lambs?

⑥ How many animals?

This baby gorilla is on
his father's back.
He loves his father.

Circle the picture.

① This is a gorilla.

② This is a puppy.

③ This is a lamb.

④ This is a kitten.

⑤ This is a rabbit.

⑥ This is a lion.

These baby birds are in
a tree. The baby birds
are looking at me.

Read aloud.

➊ This is a .

The dog has four .

➋ This is a mother .

She has a cute .

➌ This is a mother .

She has two .

➍ This is a mother .

She has three .

➎ The loves his .

15

Picture Dictionary

bird

cub

black

dog

brown

gorilla

cat

green

kitten

rabbit

lamb

sheep

lion

tree

puppy

Dolphin Readers

Dolphin Readers are available at five levels, from Starter to 4.

The Dolphins series covers four major themes:

Grammar, Living Together, The World Around Us, Science and Nature.

For each theme, there are two titles at every level.

Activity Books are available for all Dolphins.

All Dolphins are available on audio CD.
(2 TITLES ON EACH CD ☺ SEE TABLE BELOW)

Teacher's Notes are available at **www.oup.com/elt/dolphins**

	Grammar	Living Together	The World Around Us	Science and Nature
Starter	• Silly Squirrel • Monkeying Around	• My Family • A Day with Baby	• Doctor, Doctor • Moving House	• A Game of Shapes • Baby Animals
Level 1	• Meet Molly • Where Is It?	• Little Helpers • Jack the Hero	• On Safari • Lost Kitten	• Number Magic • How's the Weather?
Level 2	• Double Trouble • Super Sam	• Candy for Breakfast • Lost!	• A Visit to the City • Matt's Mistake	• Numbers, Numbers Everywhere • Circles and Squares
Level 3	• Students in Space • What Did You Do Yesterday?	• New Girl in School • Uncle Jerry's Great Idea	• Just Like Mine • Wonderful Wild Animals	• Things That Fly • Let's Go to the Rainforest
Level 4	• The Tough Task • Yesterday, Today and Tomorrow	• We Won the Cup • Up and Down	• Where People Live • City Girl, Country Boy	• In the Ocean • Go, Gorillas, Go